JOURNEY THROUGH
CHINA

LIZ GOGERLY
&
ROB HUNT

FRANKLIN WATTS
LONDON•SYDNEY

Franklin Watts

First published in Great Britain in paperback in 2018 by The Watts Publishing Group

Credits

Editor in Chief: John C. Miles

Series Editor: Amy Stephenson

Series Designer: Emma DeBanks

Picture Researcher: Diana Morris

Picture Credits: Mark Amy/Dreamstime: 6cl. Angorius/Shutterstock: 22cr. Karina Bakalyan/Dreamstime: 7bl. Paul Brighton/Shutterstock: 18br. British Library/Wikimedia: 13br. Brphoto/Dreamstime: 6tl, 9t. Dmitry Chulov/ Dreamstime: 29c. Chuya/Dreamstime: 14, 20. Andrea La Corte/Dreamstime: 18b. DK8888/Dreamstime: 4, 13t. Zhu Difeng/Shutterstock: 12-13c. Dndavis/Dreamstime: 28b. Edwardje/Dreamstime: 25b. Shannon Fagan/Dreamstime: 5b. Iakov Filmanov/Dreamstime: 7tl. Simone Gatterwi/Dreamstime: 6cr. Jose Gil/Dreamstime: 7clb. Gouyan/ Dreamstime: 24b. Hou Guima/Dreamstime: 21b. Deborah Hewitt/Dreamstime: 6c. Hulv850627/Dreamstime: 7bc. Hupeng/Dreamstime: 3b, 22-23b, 27t. imagebroker/Alamy: 8c. Imagine China/Corbis: 16. ipadimages/ Dreamstime front cover. Jiejie100/Dreamstime: 11bl. Kwokfou/Dreamstime: 8b. Liangwm/Dreamstime: 23cl. Luna Marina/Dreamstime: 7cr. Laura Lushewitz/Dreamstime: 11t. Soon Wee Meng/Dreamstime: 29t. Rutchapong Moolvai/Dreamstime: 7tcr. Mikhail Nekrasov/Dreamstime: 17tl. Nikolaoepritskii/Dreamstime: 29b. Nomad soul/ Dreamstime: 7clr. Palex66/Dreamstime: 6tcr. Panorama Stock/Robert Harding PL: 17c, 17bra. Sean Pavone/ Dreamstime: 28t. Alelsandr Penin/Dreamstime: 15t. Pengyou93/Dreamstime: 26. Photogenes: 6bl, 19t. Presse750/ Dreamstime: 7br. Dario Lo Presti/Dreamstime: 6tcl, 7cla. Segarck/Dreamstime: 7tcl. Sihasakprachum/Shutterstock: 5c. Lee Snider/Dreamstime: 27b. Johannes Gerhardus Swanepoel/Dreamstime: 7crb. Swinnear/Dreamstime: 7cl. Tao Images/Robert Harding PL: 17tr. Hein Teh/Dreamstime: 7cb. Tempestz/Dreamstime: 17br. Trudywsimmons/ Dreamstime: 21t. Venemama/Dreamstime: 19b. Ritthichai Wierakui/Dreamstime: 7tcl. Yanmingzhang/Dreamstime: 25t. Yellow River/Dreamstime: 6tr, 23cr. Xubang Yong/Dreamstime: 10-11b. Yongsky/Dreamstime: 11br. Yinan Zhang/Dreamstime: 1, 7tr, 15b. Zhanghaobeibei/Dreamstime: 24-25c.

Dewey number: 951.06
ISBN: 978 1 4451 3682 0

Printed in Malaysia

Franklin Watts
An imprint of
Hachette Children's Group
Part of The Watts Publishing Group
Carmelite House
50 Victoria Embankment
London EC4Y 0DZ

An Hachette UK Company
www.hachette.co.uk

www.franklinwatts.co.uk

CONTENTS

WELCOME TO CHINA!

Huanying ni dao Zhongguo lai! Welcome to China! Officially called the People's Republic of China, this large country in the 'Far East' has a population of 1.35 billion people, which is nearly 20 per cent of the world's total. The people of China, however, don't consider China to be in the east and they don't call their country China! Traditional Chinese maps place China at the centre of the world map and they call their country *Zhongguo* (pronounced *chunn-gwa*), which means 'middle nation'. Your journey around this vast country will take in many historic and modern aspects of China, from the urban centres of Hong Kong and Beijing, to the rice terraces of Longsheng.

The land of extremes

China lies on the world's largest continent – Asia – and it is the world's third biggest country by land area. Despite its vast size, which covers 9.6 million square km, it only has one time zone, but it does have a wide range of habitats and climates from the cold Gobi Desert – the largest desert in Asia – to the sub-tropical rainforests in the south.

▶ The Gobi Desert is slowly expanding, in a process called desertification.

Language and culture

Around 90 per cent of the Chinese population consider themselves to be of the Han majority. The other 10 per cent are made up of 55 other recognised ethnic groups, each following a wide variety of cultures, religions and philosophies.

A claim often made is that more people speak Chinese than any other language in the world. However, this is only partly true. There is no such language as Chinese, instead there is a large family of nearly 300 Chinese languages. One language, Mandarin (or Standard Chinese), is one of the 15 institutional languages of China.

Chinese languages are tonal, which means that a word with the same pronunciation can have a different meaning depending on what tone you use. In Mandarin, the word 'ma' can mean 'mother', 'scold' (to tell someone off) and 'horse' depending on the tone that is used.

A long history of invention

China is one of the oldest civilisations in the world. Throughout its long history it has been credited with some major innovations and inventions. Four of these are widely celebrated in Chinese culture: the 'Four Great Inventions' of Ancient China are paper, printing, gunpowder and the compass (the one that helps you find which direction you are facing, not the one that draws circles).

▲ In towns and cities, many Chinese people make short journeys by bicycle.

JOURNEY PLANNER

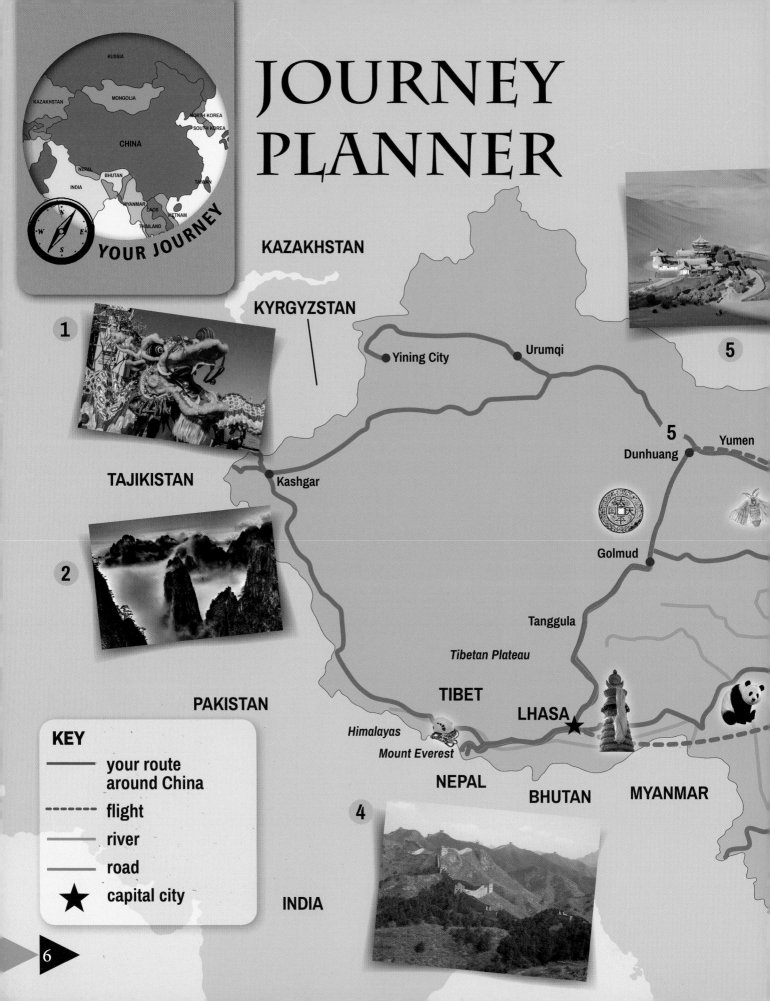

YOUR JOURNEY

RUSSIA
KAZAKHSTAN
MONGOLIA
NORTH KOREA
SOUTH KOREA
CHINA
NEPAL
BHUTAN
INDIA
TAIWAN
MYANMAR
LAOS
VIETNAM
THAILAND

KAZAKHSTAN

KYRGYZSTAN

1

Yining City   Urumqi

5

TAJIKISTAN

Kashgar

5

Dunhuang   Yumen

2

Golmud

Tanggula

Tibetan Plateau

PAKISTAN

TIBET

LHASA

Himalayas

Mount Everest

NEPAL

BHUTAN   **MYANMAR**

KEY

————	your route around China
- - - - -	flight
————	river
————	road
★	capital city

4

INDIA

RUSSIA

MONGOLIA

Qiqihar   Daqing

Harbin ⊚

Mudanjiang

Changchun

Jilin

Fuxin   Shenyang ⊚   Yanbian

Zhangjiakou

4

Datong

BEIJING

Tianjin ⊚   Dalian

NORTH KOREA

Baoding

Sea of Japan

Dongying   Yantai

Shijiazhuang

xia Landform
ngye   Gobi Desert

Yinchuan

Yellow river

3

Taiyuan ⊚   Zibo ⊚

Jinan

SOUTH KOREA   JAPAN

Xining   Lanzhou

Zhengzhou

Xuzhou

Xianyang ⊚   Qufu

Xi'an

Hefei   Nanjing

East China Sea

Mianyang

Suizhou

Wuhan ⊚   **2**   Suzhou   Shanghai ⊚

Chengdu ⊚   Chongqing

Huangshan   Hangzhou

Neijiang   Changde

Ningbo

Jingdezhen

Wenzhou

Yangtze river   Changsha   Nanchang

Zhaotong

Guiyang   Hengyang   Fuzhou

6

6

Qujing   Guilin

Meizhou

Kunming   Liuzhou   Shaoguan   Xiamen

Guangzhou   Shantou

TAIWAN

Nanning   Shenzhen ⊚

Macao   Hong Kong   **1**

AOS

VIETNAM   South China Sea

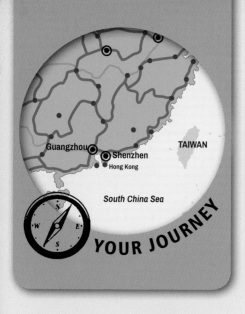

HONG KONG

The great ancient Chinese philosopher, Laozi, said, 'A journey of a thousand miles begins with a single step.' Your journey will be a lot further than a thousand miles, and from your start in Hong Kong you will have some amazing technology and infrastructures to help you get around.

Happy landings

Your first step will be off the plane at Hong Kong International Airport, located on the man-made island of Chek Lap Kok. Be glad that you are landing here and not at the old Kai Tak airport. Hong Kong is spread over 200 islands, and pilots coming in to Kai Tak had to negotiate mountains and fly perilously close to surrounding skyscrapers to land on a runway that stretched into the waters of Kowloon Bay. Occasionally, planes overran the runway and ended up in the water! No wonder it was once listed as one of the world's most dangerous airports.

▼ Planes flew incredibly close to Hong Kong's buildings when taking off and landing at Kai Tak airport.

British connection

Before 1 July 1997, a trip to Hong Kong would not have been a trip to China. This is because for the previous 156 years it was governed as a British colony. The British won Hong Kong from China after a series of wars in the 19th century, but negotiations to return it to China began in the 1970s. You will find various streets and places named after historic British figures, such as Prince Edward Road and Wellington Street, but the most notable is probably Victoria Harbour, named after Queen Victoria (1819–1901). It is well worth taking a cruise around the harbour to see the city at its best. Cruise in the evening, and you'll see the world's biggest permanent light show – A Symphony of Lights (see page 8).

New Year in February?

New Year celebrations in Hong Kong are considered to be some of the most spectacular on the planet, but don't expect to see them on 31 December! Although the Chinese use the same calendar as Western nations for business, for cultural events they use the Chinese calendar, which is based on the phases of the Moon. This means that Chinese New Year can take place anytime between the end of January and mid-February. Expect to see parades, Chinese dragons (see above, right), horse races and plenty of fireworks.

▲ Chinese dragons are a symbol of China. They represent power, wisdom and good luck.

Made in Hong Kong

Hong Kong has a long tradition of manufacturing. In 1949, when China became a communist nation, an influx of refugees and wealthy businessmen turned Hong Kong into a boomtown. Plastic manufacturing and the toy industry peaked between 1948 and the 1970s, and many plastic dolls, cars and other toys were stamped with 'Made in Hong Kong'. The electronics and watchmaking industries took off in the 1970s, but by the 1980s many manufacturers had relocated to China. In the 21st century Hong Kong has established itself as a major centre for publishing and printing.

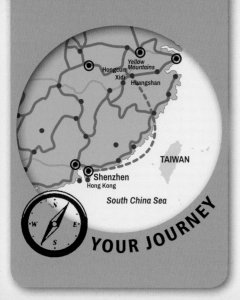

YOUR JOURNEY

HONG KONG TO HUANGSHAN

To reach your next destination you should first travel to Shenzhen either by Metro, by bus or by the SkyPier Ferry. You will need a visa because Shenzhen is a 'Special Economic Zone'. This means it has different employment and trade laws to other parts of China, which helps it trade internationally much more effectively. From Shenzhen, a plane whisks you to the fabulous sights of Huangshan in around 2 hours.

▲ The Yellow Mountains aren't actually yellow. They are named after the 'Yellow Emperor', Huangdi (c.2697– c.2598 BCE).

'Loveliest mountains in China'

Huangshan means 'Yellow Mountains', but this description does not do this amazing mountain range justice. As you gaze in wonder at the strange, granite peaks, rising above the clouds, some of it may feel familiar. That is because, for centuries, these mountains have inspired all sorts of artworks; particularly Chinese ink painting. They have had countless poems written about them and even have a school of art named after them. Their glory is such that one peak is called 'Beginning-to-Believe', after the legend of a traveller who had doubted the mountains could be as beautiful as he'd been told. If you are lucky enough to see the sun set from above the clouds, you will understand how he felt.

Living history

A great way to get a feel for China's history is to visit the traditional villages of Xidi and Hongcun. Set in the foothills of the mountains, these 900-year-old communes provide an insight into the past and are protected by UNESCO. Hongcun is actually set out in the shape of an ox (a domesticated cow or bull). The villagers consider the head and horns to be represented by a hill and two trees. The body is where the houses are and the streams that run through the village are the ox's intestines! Both Hongcun and Xidi have beautiful examples of old wooden buildings carved in a traditional local style.

◀ Tea is often served in china – a type of porcelain (baked clay) so-called because it was first made in China.

Time for tea

Tea is extremely important to the Chinese, both culturally and economically, as they are the world's biggest producers and drinkers of tea. Two of the most popular teas, Maofeng and Keemun, are grown in the Huangshan area. There are rules to be followed when drinking tea in China – your host will always keep topping up your cup so that it never runs dry. You must thank them by tapping two bent fingers on the table.

▲ The houses in the village of Hongcun form the body of the 'ox'.

▶ A traditional timber-framed building in Xidi.

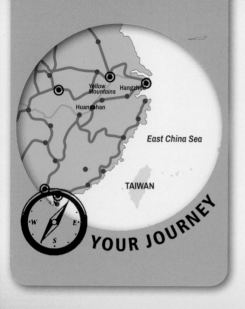

YOUR JOURNEY

HUANGSHAN TO HANGZHOU

Driving around China is difficult for tourists because the authorities only accept Chinese driving licences. Getting one of these for your trip is possible but tricky. However, this may not be a bad thing because driving in China is notoriously dangerous and the death rate on the roads is catastrophic. It's safer, and reasonably cheap, to hire an experienced driver for your 442-km journey to Hangzhou.

▼ The Qiantang river flows past the Economic and Technological Development Zones, and into the East China Sea at Hangzhou Bay.

An ancient capital

Hangzhou is regarded as one of the 'Seven Ancient Capitals of China', as it was the main city of the Wuyue Kingdom more than 1,000 years ago. At that time China was a group of kingdoms that sometimes managed to co-operate with each other, but more often fought with one another. Today it is a mixture of ancient wonders and modern industries, many of which are located in the Economic and Technological Development Zones. To get about you can hire a bike from Hangzhou Public Bicycle, the largest bike-sharing system in the world.

While you are here you must visit the Liuhe ('Six Harmonies') Pagoda, which sits close to the Qiantang river. A pagoda has existed on this site since 970 CE. The pagoda used to serve as a lighthouse – a lantern would be placed at the top to guide boats along the river.

11th-century genius

Another place to visit is the tomb of the incredible Shen Kuo (1031–1095). It would take a full book to list all the accomplishments of Shen Kuo. He was a politician, an astronomer, a weatherman, a chemist, a map-maker and an inventor – to name just a few things he was good at! Probably his most famous achievement was to develop the magnetic compass for navigation. This humble device can reliably tell you where north and south are. This simple bit of knowledge allowed explorers to journey across the seas to visit unknown parts of the world and also find their way back home.

▶ A statue of Shen Kuo – a man of many talents.

The original printing press

Shen Kuo also wrote *The Dream Pool Essays*, which is the main source for the story of Bi Sheng (990–1051), the creator of another of the Four Great Inventions. Sheng was a worker who used porcelain to make movable type blocks – the small blocks with raised impressions of letters and characters that are used to create printed words when inked and pressed onto paper. This made mass-printing possible nearly 400 years before Johannes Gutenberg (c. 1398–1468) developed his printing press in Europe in the 15th century.

▲ An extract from the Chinese version of the *Diamond Sutra* – the earliest printed book.

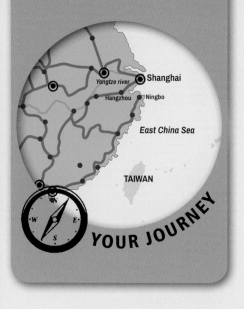

HANGZHOU TO SHANGHAI

The next stage of your journey, to Shanghai, is one of the shortest at around 193 km. You could take a car, perhaps a Xialong Fierce Dragon, which is a Chinese-made version of a Hummer Jeep, and do the journey in a couple of hours. If time is an issue, travel by high-speed train and, at world-record speeds of more than 400 kph, do it in as little as 45 minutes!

Surprising Shanghai

If you measure Shanghai by the population within the city limits, it has over 24 million inhabitants! This makes Shanghai the biggest city on Earth. It's also China's commercial and financial capital, the location of one of China's stock exchanges and home to several of China's leading airline and shipping companies.

The name Shanghai means 'above the sea' and the shores around the city are the best places to be if you want a bit of beach-time. Dedicated swimmers should travel out to one of the many beaches that overlook the East China Sea, but if you just want a paddle, visit the artificial beach at the Bund on the Huangpu river.

▼ The Bund is a fashionable inner-city waterfront area in Shanghai, and is very popular with tourists.

◀ A cargo ship ferrying building materials along the Yangtze river.

The Yangtze

The Huangpu river might look big from the beach, but it is a minor tributary of one of the world's great rivers – the Yangtze. Yangtze means 'long' and it is the third longest river on the planet. The river rises in the glaciers of the Tanggula Mountains, near Tibet, and travels nearly 6,437 km to its mouth on the East China Sea, just north of Shanghai city centre.

The river is extremely important to China's economy, and it is one of the busiest rivers in the world, carrying people, fuel and goods. Unfortunately, it has become so terribly polluted that the baiji dolphin, which is unique to the Yangtze, has recently been declared extinct and other species, such as the Chinese paddlefish, are under threat. It is also where you will find the Three Gorges Dam, which at 2.25 km long and 185 m high is the world's largest power station. At one point it provided 10 per cent of China's electricity.

Magic magnetic travel

A really quick way to get from the city centre to the airport is on the Shanghai Maglev Train. It is so fast that it covers the 30.5-km distance in just 8 minutes. Maglev is short for 'magnetic levitation' and the train uses powerful magnets to levitate (hover) above the track. It is the lack of friction that this levitation causes that makes the trains so fast.

▼ A world-leading city like Shanghai needs fast transport connections to help its businesses connect with international visitors.

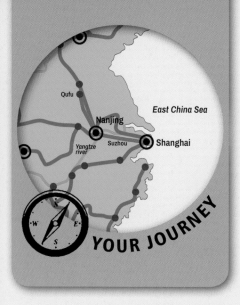

Qufu

East China Sea

Nanjing

Yangtze river

Suzhou

Shanghai

SHANGHAI TO SUZHOU AND QUFU

You can leave the car behind for the next part of your journey. You are about to jump on the Jinghu High-Speed Railway, which happens to be the longest high speed track in the world. The train will eventually take you to the capital city of China, Beijing. Before you reach Beijing you must stop off and visit the historic cities of Suzhou and Qufu, which are conveniently placed on the same railway line.

Supertrain

The Jinghu High-Speed Railway is also known as the Beijing-Shanghai route as it links these two great cities. The journey is 1,305 km long and can be completed in just 3 hours and 58 minutes. Before you reach your first stop in Suzhou, you will cross the Danyang-Kunshan Grand Bridge, which opened in 2011. At a whopping 164.8 km long, this is the longest bridge of any kind in the world.

▶ The Danyang-Kunshan Grand Bridge has a 9-km long section that crosses the Yangcheng Lake.

▲ Tourists take a ride along one of Suzhou's many waterways.

Suzhou

At 2,500 years old, Suzhou is one of China's oldest cities and is considered to be one of the most beautiful. It used to be a holiday destination for the Chinese nobility and is famous for the gardens that were created for them. One of the biggest and best is the Humble Administrator's Garden, built in 1509. Here you can walk amongst beautifully constructed landscapes filled with lotus pools and ponds full of Mandarin ducks.

The city of Suzhou is often compared to Venice in Italy. This is because it is home to a series of water towns; traditional villages where old wooden houses seemingly float on the canals that fill the landscape. The best of these villages is perhaps Tongli. You can take a boat ride around the waterways to see the town's incredibly well-preserved buildings.

Confucius of Qufu

Your next stop on the line is at another ancient city, Qufu, the home of Confucius. Confucius was a philosopher who lived from 551–479 BCE. His ideas of education, hard work and the collective responsibility of everybody to make a good society are extremely influential to this day. Before he died he thought he had failed to make an impact, but after his death his teachings became more and more popular and shaped how China developed as a nation. Be sure to visit the three Confucian sites known as the *San Kong*: the mansion he lived in, the temple he worshipped at and the cemetery in which he is buried.

◄ Mansion

▶ Temple

◄ Cemetery

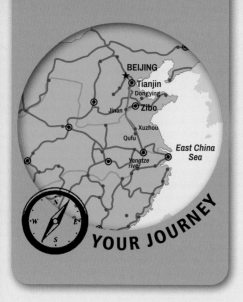

YOUR JOURNEY

QUFU TO BEIJING

Get the fastest long-distance train (a G-train) from Qufu train station, and treat yourself to a business-class, sightseeing seat. The seating system on Chinese trains gives you an insight into how Chinese people view life and work, as the seats in business class are much better than first-class! The leather sightseeing seats are only available on some trains, but they are very luxurious and swivel round so you can take in the views through the extra-large windows on your 2-hour journey.

The Northern Capital

The Chinese have a habit of giving places very obvious names and Beijing, meaning 'the Northern Capital' is no exception. The name might be a bit dull, but the city certainly isn't. China's second-biggest city certainly has history – prehistoric remains of early humans have been found here that date back 250,000 years! The city itself developed more than 3,000 years ago, so there is plenty to discover. You would need a few weeks to explore it properly, but when time is limited there are a few sights that are absolutely essential. These include the Summer Palace, the Forbidden City, Tiananmen Square and, of course, the longest and most famous wall ever built!

▼ The Hall of Supreme Harmony sits in the centre of the Forbidden City.

Peking duck

China has a huge variety of cuisines, but you can't visit Beijing without trying Peking duck (see below). Peking was the word used by westerners to pronounce the name of the capital city. The Chinese eat more duck meat than any other country in the world. Peking duck is roasted, thinly sliced, and then served with pancakes, sweet bean sauce and spring onions – it is delicious!

The Great Wall of China

The Chinese name for the world's largest man-made structure is *Wanli Changcheng*, or 'the Long Wall'. The wall is actually a series of structures built over many centuries to protect China from invasion. The oldest bits of the wall date from the 7th century BCE, and over time the different parts were joined up to form an incredible piece of architecture. It stretches 21,195 km from east to west, but some of its best parts, built in the 14th century during the Ming Dynasty, are just an hour's journey from Beijing.

Chairman Mao

Mao Zedong (1893–1976), along with Confucius (see page 17), is the other personality that greatly affected the Chinese way of life. Better known as Chairman Mao, he was a leader of the Communist Party of China, which has ruled the country since 1949. He is still considered by many in China to be a great leader and there are always long lines outside his mausoleum in Tiananmen Square, where his body has been lying in state, in a crystal coffin, since his death in 1976. A short walk away from this is the Forbidden City, a series of ancient wooden buildings that was once home to the emperors that ruled China.

China's most visited

Tourism in China is growing quickly and Beijing has three of the top 50 most-visited attractions in the world.

16. The Forbidden City. This palace gets its name from the fact that people weren't allowed to enter or leave without the emperor's permission.
Annual Visitors: 15,340,000

26. The Great Wall of China
Annual Visitors: 10,720,000

46. The National Museum of China.
Annual Visitors: 7,450,000

Mao Zedong held the office of Chairman between 1945 and 1976. This portrait of him hangs in Tiananmen Square.

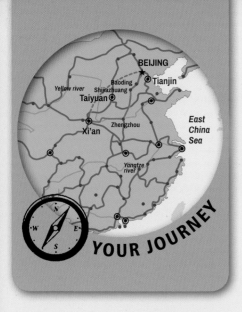

YOUR JOURNEY

BEIJING TO XI'AN

Beijing has its fair share of history, but your next destination, Xi'an, has even more! You could fly there in 2 hours, but it's much more fun to take the overnight 'soft sleeper' train. The cheaper cabins have four bunk beds in them, so take earplugs because you'll probably have to share. If you want more privacy, you can pay extra for a deluxe two-bed cabin and snooze in peace for the 12-hour journey.

Silk city

With over 3,000 years of history, it's little wonder that Xi'an is known as 'the birthplace of Chinese civilisation'. It was a capital city of ten of China's ruling families, known as dynasties, and is also the start of 'the Silk Road' – the ancient trading route that linked China to the West. During the Tang Dynasty (618-907 CE), Xi'an – then known as Chang'an – was probably the biggest city in the world and was an important centre for culture and commerce. Today Xi'an is still a major player in China's economy, with expertise in manufacturing, technology and software engineering.

The best place to visit to learn more about Xi'an's long history is the city's Shaanxi History Museum. After that, pop in to the nearby Big Wild Goose Pagoda. First built in 589 CE, it's one of China's oldest and most beautiful buildings. For stunning views of the city, take a cycle tour of the city wall. You can hire a bike from any of the four gates in the wall.

▶ Xi'an's old city wall sits alongside modern high-rise apartment blocks and offices.

> The Terracotta Army can be visited at the Qin Shi Huang Mausoleum.

The Terracotta Army of Qin Shi Huang

One of the most important archaeological discoveries of all time was made here in 1974 when some farmers started digging a well to the east of the city. Instead of water, they found an underground army – made from clay! The Terracotta Army, as it came to be known, was a group of around 6,000 soldiers constructed on the orders of Qin Shi Huang (c.259–210 BCE), the first emperor of China.

The figures were manufactured using an assembly line method and each of the figures is slightly different. Along with the figures were weapons, armour and even chariots with horses. The army was completed by 210 BCE. Qin died after drinking a potion that was supposed to make him live forever. The soldiers were then buried surrounding Qin's tomb, presumably to defend him in the afterlife.

The big bang

Emperor Qin wasn't the only one obsessed with eternal life: for centuries emperors encouraged chemical experiments to try to find a way to cheat death. They didn't succeed, but in the 9th century CE, when Xi'an was the capital of the Tang Dynasty, an experimenter finally mixed together the chemicals to make gunpowder – another of the Four Great Chinese inventions. Gunpowder was the first explosive material and was initially used to make fireworks. Today, China makes and exports more fireworks than any other country in the world.

◀ Fireworks were a feature of the opening ceremony of the 2008 Beijing Olympics.

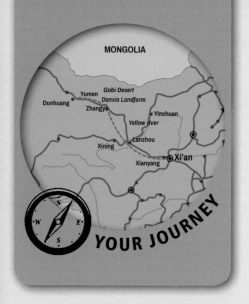

YOUR JOURNEY

THE SILK ROAD

The next stage of your journey follows the path of the ancient trading route: the Silk Road. This ancient trading route runs 6,437 km from China to Europe and crosses the Gobi Desert.

Travelling from Xi'an to Dunhuang

Centuries ago, groups of merchants would take months to make the journey through the desert, fearful of attack from bandits. The quickest form of transport back then was the Bactrian camel. Today, if money is no object, you can travel in style in your own private jet! Despite being a Communist country, some Chinese are now extremely wealthy. In 2015 it had the most billionaires in the world after the USA, and many companies have sprung up to cater for the demand for private jet travel.

▶ A caravan of Bactrian camels, which have two distinctive humps.

Secret of silk

The ancient Silk Road got its name from a mysterious and beautiful cloth that was first made in China – silk. For centuries silk was highly prized, mainly because no one outside of China had a clue about how it was made. Eventually the secret got out and people realised that they were actually wearing beautiful cloth made from the cocoons of the silkworm moth (see below).

Zhangye and Danxia

Your first jet-stop is the small city of Zhangye near the border of China and Inner Mongolia. The Giant Buddha Temple here is supposedly the birthplace of the fearsome Mongol, Emperor, Kublai Khan (1215–1294).

Nearby is the Danxia Landform. It is a geological phenomenon only found in China. It is the result of red sandstone and other mineral deposits being laid down over millions of years. The layers were then warped and twisted by the same tectonic plates that created the Himalayan Mountains. (The Himalayas lie along China's border with India.) The result is rock formations so strange and colourful (see below) that you might think your eyes are playing tricks on you!

Beautiful oasis

Your jet ride ends in Dunhuang, which sits in an oasis in the Gobi Desert. It contains the beautiful Crescent Lake (see below) and the singing mountain, Mingsha Shan, also known as the 'Echoing Sand Mountain'. If the wind is blowing you will hear the sand begin to resonate and hum. This is the time to jump aboard 'the ship of the desert' – the camel, as before you leave the desert you must take a tour to the Mogao Caves, the site of another great archaeological discovery. The caves were carved in the 4th century and contain some stunning ancient Buddhist artwork, including statues and murals.

Gobi Desert facts

Gobi means 'waterless place'.

The first scientifically recognised dinosaur eggs ever found were discovered here.

It is classed as a cold desert. Temperatures range between -47°C in winter to 38.6°C in summer. It can even snow here in the winter!

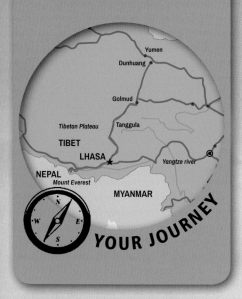

YOUR JOURNEY

LHASA

The next stage of the trip is a big one and not at all easy. First of all, you need special visas to visit the Tibet Autonomous Region. An autonomous region gets to make some of its own laws and two of the rules are that tourists must be in groups and be directed by a travel guide. From Dunhuang you will need to take a bus to the city of Golmud, but from there you can take the Qinghai-Tibet Railway to complete your 1,686-km trip.

▼ A train passes through the 2.5 million square km of the Tibetan Plateau.

The railway above the clouds

At 4,000 m above sea level, the Qinghai-Tibet Railway is a miracle of engineering. Many experts thought it would be impossible to construct because of the cold and lack of oxygen at this high altitude. It is the world's highest railway, and each passenger has a personal oxygen supply. The scenery is amazing and you will stop at the world's highest railway station (Tanggula) and go through the world's highest railway tunnel – the Fenghuoshan Tunnel.

▲ Yaks are a traditional form of transport in Tibet. Due to the lack of trees this high above sea level, yak dung is burnt as fuel!

Lhasa

Lhasa, in the Himalayan region, is the capital of the Tibet region and, at nearly 3,500 metres above sea level, some people can become ill because the air is so thin. Once you are used to it, the city is a fascinating place. The name Lhasa means 'place of the gods' – the city is full of important Buddhist artefacts and buildings. Easily the most impressive of these is the Potala Palace.

▼ Locals shopping at a market in Lhasa.

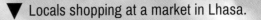

▼ A view of Mount Everest from the base camp in Tibet. The colourful flags are Buddhist prayer flags.

Potala Palace

The Potala Palace is a fabulous 13-storey, 1,000-room castle that sits on a rock overlooking a beautiful park with a lake. It was built in the 17th century and became the residence of the Tibetan Buddhist leaders: the Dalai Lamas. Each Dalai Lama is supposedly a reincarnation of the one before. A new Dalai Lama is located by a group of followers who look for clues. The current Dalai Lama was chosen at the age of two because the followers showed him the previous Lama's possessions and he cried out 'it's mine!'. He was exiled in 1959, after an uprising, which means he now has to live in another country: India.

Mount Everest and the Himalayas

Mount Everest, the world's highest mountain, is located in the majestic mountain range of the Himalayas, and although it's a 2-day car journey from Lhasa to Everest's base camp, it's worth it to see Chomolungma as the locals call it. It's probably safer to stay at base camp and enjoy the view, as there are an estimated 200 dead bodies still on the mountain – the remains of climbers who've either fallen or succumbed to altitude sickness.

25

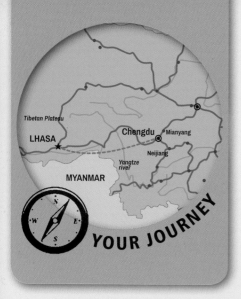

YOUR JOURNEY

LHASA TO CHENGDU

It's time to head back east, so take a 2-hour plane ride from Lhasa to Chengdu. Don't be put off by the weather (Chengdu is famous for its drizzle) – this 2,000-year-old city has a lot going for it: culture, cuisine, but most of all, pandas!

Marco Polo to the present day

Marco Polo was a merchant from Venice who travelled around China in the 13th century. His written tales of his journeys were the first accounts of China read by Europeans. He visited Chengdu and wrote admiringly of the Anshun Bridge. There is a different bridge crossing the Jin river now, but it is still beautiful and has a very popular restaurant.

While you're in Chengdu you should visit the New Century Global Center. It currently holds the record for being the world's largest building and has everything from an ice rink and water park to hotels, restaurants and a shopping centre. And, it would certainly have given Marco Polo something to write home about!

▼ Beneath the curved roof of the New Century Global Center is over 1.7 million square m of floor space.

▶ Deforestation has destroyed much of the giant panda's natural habitat.

Perfect for pandas

The giant panda is one of the world's most beloved animals and they only live in China's mountainous bamboo forests. Sadly there are less than 2,000 giant pandas left in the wild. A visit to Chengdu's Panda Breeding and Research Centre not only gives you the chance to see these beautiful creatures up close, but also helps fund attempts to save the species. There is also a zoo nearby where you can see another endangered animal – the South China tiger.

Fabulous food

You will be able to find tasty Chinese food wherever you go on your journey, but this is the place to taste spicy Szechuan food. Make sure you try the famous *huo guo*, a peppery 'hot pot' broth that could blow your socks off! Another favourite is *dandan mian* – the name means 'noodles carried on a pole' and refers to the way the street sellers used to carry the bowls of noodles and sauce – balanced at either end of a pole and carried over their shoulder.

▶ Sampling the delicious food from street vendors is a highlight of any visit to Chengdu.

Giant panda facts

Even though 99 per cent of their diet is bamboo, giant pandas are actually classed as meat eaters – they will sometimes eat small animals.

Scientists used to think the giant panda was more like a racoon than a bear, but it's now back to being a bear again!

The two great problems with giant pandas is feeding them and getting them to breed. They mostly eat bamboo (up to 38 kg a day) and the females can only become pregnant on two days of the year.

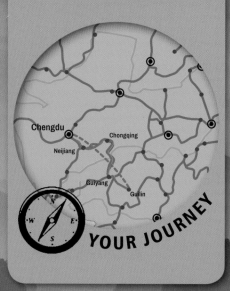

YOUR JOURNEY

CHENGDU TO GUILIN

Your long journey began with a single step but sadly it must soon end. At least make sure you end it in a place of great beauty – the city of Guilin. It's a 1 hour 40 minute flight from Chengdu, but if you want to see more countryside and are prepared to brave the Chinese roads, then why not drive in luxury in a Volvo S60 Inscription. You might think that Volvo is a Swedish brand, but it is owned by the Chinese company Geely and made in Chengdu. It is also the first Chinese-built car to be sold in the USA.

▲ The distinctive rock towers of Guilin are a famous Chinese landmark.

Karst country

If you look at the back of a 20 Yuan Chinese bank note (see below), you will see an image of what appears to be some kind of bizarre science-fiction landscape: strange peaks tower over a tiny boat on a river. This fantastic landscape isn't on another planet, it's actually in Guilin and the exotic peaks were caused by millions of years-worth of slightly acidic rain, which dissolved the soft rock, leaving tougher rock behind in the form of tall towers. It is known as 'Karst topography' and the examples in Gulin are amongst the most dramatic on the planet.

Li river cruise

The river depicted on the banknote is the Li river and the best view of those amazing Karst peaks is from one of the famous Li river cruise ships (see right). If you prefer something more traditional and less crowded then you can hire a bamboo raft instead. If you don't fancy the river, hiring a bicycle is another great way to see the area. Until recently, the humble bike was the main form of transport for short distances, but nowadays more and more people are taking to their cars. As a result, many cities in China now have terrible problems with pollution; fortunately, Guilin is not yet one of them.

Longsheng rice terraces

For more outlandish landscapes, take a 100-km trip north to see the Longsheng rice terraces, also known as the 'Dragon's Backbone'. These terraces wind around the mountains from the river and are said to resemble the scales of a dragon. Their appearance depends on the time of year: in spring they are flooded with water; in summer filled with green rice shoots; in autumn full of rice plants; and in winter layered with frost. As you pass through the Huangluo village you will see that it is the custom of the Yao women from this region to wear their hair as long as possible.

▲ Some Yao women grow their hair as long as 2 metres! It is wound around the head to keep it out of the way.

▼ Small villages nestle amongst the lush rice terraces.

GLOSSARY

administrator
A person who organises things in business.

altitude sickness
An illness that happens when someone is high above sea level, where oxygen levels are low.

archaeology
The study of history by examining items from the past.

artefacts
A man-made object, usually of cultural or historical importance.

astronomy
The study of the stars and planets.

autonomous
Freedom to control.

Buddha
The founder of the Buddhist religion, believed to have lived either c.563–483 BCE or c.480–400 BCE.

Buddhist
A follower of the religion of Buddhism, based on the teachings of Buddha.

caravan
In this instance, a group of travellers crossing a desert.

catastrophic
Causing great damage.

climate
The average weather conditions in a particular area.

cocoon
A silky case spun by some insect larvae.

colony
A country or area under the control of another country.

commerce
Buying and selling things.

commune
A group of people living and working together and sharing some possessions.

communism
A society where all property is owned by the community.

deforestation
When a large area of trees is cleared.

dynasty
A line of rulers of a country who come from the same family.

ethnic
The culture, traditions and beliefs of a smaller group within a larger population.

Han
The Chinese dynasty that ruled from 206 BCE to 220 CE.

humble
Showing a modest or low opinion of your own importance.

innovation
Coming up with new ideas.

lying in state
When a corpse is put on public display before it is buried or cremated.

mausoleum
A building that contains the remains of dead people.

medieval
The 'Middle Ages' in Europe from the 5th to the 15th centuries.

merchant
A person who provides goods for a price.

Ming
The Chinese dynasty that ruled from 1368–1644.

Mongol
A person from Mongolia.

negotiate
To reach an agreement or find a way through something.

oasis
A place in a desert where water is found.

pagoda
A Buddhist temple, often in the form of a tower with many tiers.

philosophy
The study of knowledge, reality and existence.

reincarnation
The belief that after death one is reborn.

republic
A country or state where power is held by the people and their elected representatives, such as a president, rather than a monarch.

resonate
A deep, full sound.

sub-tropical
Regions of the Earth that are just outside the Tropic of Cancer and the Tropic of Capricorn. Most of the world's deserts lie in the sub-tropics.

symphony
An elaborate composition of different elements, usually of music.

Tang
The Chinese dynasty that ruled from 618– c.906 CE.

tectonic plates
The separate plates that make up the crust of the Earth.

tonal language
A language where different pitch tones change the meaning of the word.

topography
The arrangement of the geographical features of an area.

tributary
A river or stream flowing into a larger river or lake.

UNESCO
A United Nations agency that promotes the exchange of culture, ideas and information.

urban
Of a town or city.